THE THOUGHT LOG
Cognitive Behavioral Therapy to Process and Reframe

Designed by therapists to challenge
unhelpful thought patterns.

. . . .
(THIS BOOK BELONGS TO)

. . . .
(IF FOUND, PLEASE RETURN TO)

LEARN MORE
www.therapynotebooks.com

THERAPY NOTEBOOKS
Published by Subject Matters

ISBN: 9781958963029
Printed in the United States of America

LEAD THERAPIST
Diana Hu, PsyD

EDITED BY
Jake Abrahamson

DESIGNED BY
Monumento.Co

BRANDING BY
High Tide

IF YOU ARE IN URGENT
NEED OF ASSISTANCE:
Dial 9-1-1

FOR MENTAL HEALTH
CRISIS SUPPORT:
Dial 9-8-8

SAMHSA National Helpline
1-800-622-HELP (4357)

Crisis Text Line
Text HOME to 741741

PUBLISHER'S NOTE:
This publication is not therapy or a replacement for therapy with a licensed professional. It is designed to provide information in regard to the subject matter covered. It is sold with the understanding that the publisher is not engaged in rendering psychological, financial, legal, or other professional services. If expert assistance or counseling is needed, the services of a competent professional should be sought.

Copyright © 2023 Subject Matters. All rights reserved. All material in this notebook may not be reproduced, transmitted, or distributed in any form without the written permission of Subject Matters.

Some Guiding Principles

This journal is designed for you to start right away if you wish. You can do that by going to Your Journal Entries on page 30. For additional context on key definitions and the evidence behind this journal, flip to the Resource Guide. Over the next page, we share a few guiding principles that will help you get the most out of this book.

1   What is the purpose of this journal?

        The Thought Log is a tool that helps you build awareness of the relationship between your thoughts, feelings, and behaviors. As your understanding of this relationship grows, you'll become empowered to reframe unhelpful thoughts and improve how you feel—both in the moment and in the future. Rooted in Cognitive Behavioral Therapy (considered by many to be the "gold standard" in psychotherapy), this tool contains thirty journal entries from our popular *The Anti-Anxiety Notebook*, alongside brand new Notes From a Therapist and a handy Resource Guide for those who want a primer on CBT.

2   When should I use this journal?

        Whenever you feel the need—whether that's on a set schedule, or in response to triggering thoughts, feelings, or events.

3   What do I need to know to get started?

        Nothing—you can dive right in. The journal entries provide clear instructions and don't require any background knowledge in psychology or CBT. With that said, the Resource Guide does include some basic context around CBT that can help you better understand what the entries are asking you and why. You can read this before starting your entries, or you can get started and refer to it as needed.

How This Book Helps You

1. Practice clinical psychology's "gold standard" for challenging a variety of unhelpful, negative thought patterns: Cognitive Behavioral Therapy.

   The Thought Log uses Cognitive Behavioral Therapy to help you neutralize the thought patterns that drive anxiety, stress, depression, and other mental health difficulties. This effective, thoroughly researched form of psychotherapy can be helpful to anyone, even if you don't have a mental health diagnosis.

2. You don't need any prior experience with CBT, therapy, or journaling. If you have difficult thoughts and feelings, this product is for you.

   Even if you've never been to therapy or have never heard of CBT, you'll be able to start immediately. This journal contains just enough guidance to help you make the most of the entries, without your having to wade through pages and pages of technical jargon.

3. The right amount of structure and freedom to support your journaling.

   A blank page can feel paralyzing, but too many prompts can be daunting, too. These journal entries—utilized effectively by thousands of users of *The Anti-Anxiety Notebook*—are structured enough to help you process your thoughts and feelings, and open-ended enough to apply to a variety of situations.

4. Made by therapists who have helped countless clients put this tool into practice.

   The expert behind *The Thought Log* has years of experience using this tool to help clients combat unhelpful thought patterns. They've distilled key clinical practices into simple tips to help you build new insight through journaling.

Scan the QR code to meet our experts

Contents

10	I	RESOURCE GUIDE
12		Cognitive Behavioral Therapy Basics
20		Cognitive Distortions
28		The Feelings Wheel
30	II	YOUR JOURNAL ENTRIES
32		Tips & Setting Intentions
34		Journal Entry Guide & Sample Entry
42		Entries 1–10
84		Journal Synthesis
86		Entries 11–20
128		Journal Synthesis
130		Entries 21–30
172		Journal Synthesis
174		References

I Resource Guide

Use this section to learn about Cognitive Behavioral Therapy fundamentals that may be helpful to your journaling.

Cognitive Behavioral Therapy Basics

Cognitive Behavioral Therapy (CBT) is based on a simple yet powerful insight: our thoughts drive our feelings and behavior. If we learn to change the thoughts that lead us to feel bad, then we can feel better.

A BRIEF HISTORY

Prior to the development of CBT, psychotherapy was dominated by the belief that painful feelings are caused by early childhood experiences. The path to relieving those feelings was through analysis that identified unconscious memories and associations. That branch of therapy, which is still in use today, is known as psychodynamic therapy and is probably most famous for its leading figure, Sigmund Freud.

Though CBT recognizes this connection between current feelings and early experiences, its focus is on understanding how our everyday thought patterns drive emotions and behavior. It was first developed in the 1960s when psychiatrist and researcher Aaron Beck noticed that his clients often engaged in destructive thought patterns. He reasoned that if they could change the stories they told themselves, their resulting feelings and behaviors might change too. This became the founding principle of CBT: we are governed more by our perceptions of reality than by reality itself, and so by changing our perceptions, we can feel entirely different than we did before.

Since its introduction, CBT has become the "gold standard" of psychotherapy.[1] Hundreds of studies over the last few decades have shown that CBT can be used to relieve a large variety of problems, including anxiety, depression, and chronic medical issues.[2]

THE ABC MODEL OF EMOTIONS

At its core, CBT is based on a simple concept called the ABC Model of Emotions. According to this framework, we have emotions when an Activating situation (A) triggers a Belief or thought (B), which leads to a Consequence or emotion (C). One key takeaway from this model is that an activating situation alone does not directly cause an emotional response. When we encounter a situation (A), a thought or belief (B) arises that tells us how to interpret it. After we have had this thought, we go on to have an emotional response (C).

For instance, if you get stuck in traffic, you might react by thinking, "I'm going to be late for work and my boss will think I'm irresponsible." Or you may think, "This is bad luck, but there is nothing I can do about it." The former thought leads to feelings of worry, stress, and fear, whereas the latter thought leads to a feeling of acceptance.

Much of the work of CBT involves paying close attention to the interactions between A, B, and C that we experience everyday. By developing an awareness of our most common ABC patterns, we can begin to challenge our unhelpful thoughts and guide our emotional responses.

AUTOMATIC THOUGHTS

The thoughts we have during the B phase of the ABC process tend to be automatic. In other words, we do not intentionally think these thoughts—they arise on their own in response to a situation, and in many cases this happens so rapidly that we don't even realize we're having them. They're usually influenced by how we've experienced similar situations in the past.

For example, you may have once been bitten by a dog, which led you to think of dogs as dangerous. Now when you encounter a large dog, an automatic thought tells you that the situation is dangerous and you should walk away. Or perhaps you once had a boss who emailed you only when you did things wrong. Now you have a new boss who gives lots of praise at a new job that you love, but you still have a belief that emails from the boss are bad news, and that's the thought that pops into your head when you see your new boss's name in your inbox.

Automatic thoughts can be helpful shortcuts. (Imagine the effort it would take to sit down and deliberately assess every stimulus, situation, or event we encounter in our daily lives). But they can also cause us to experience the world through an inaccurate, unnecessarily negative lens. Not every canine encounter needs to trigger a feeling of danger, and the mere appearance of an email from the boss doesn't necessarily warrant a stressful response. When automatic thoughts are inaccurate and unhelpful, they fall under the broad category of Cognitive Distortions. You can read more about the common types of cognitive distortions in the next section of the Resource Guide.

We counter automatic thoughts and cognitive distortions by revisiting the situation and reinterpreting it through a more accurate lens. You'll read more about how to do this in the Journal Entry Guide.

FEEDBACK LOOPS

Your thoughts and feelings create powerful feedback loops: you likely have thoughts about your emotional reactions, which lead to additional thoughts and reactions. (For example: "Because I thought, 'I can't be late!' I started to panic, and this made me think I can't possibly be doing a good job if I'm panicking all the time.") In this way, the ABC process doesn't stop at C, but goes on to spawn further ABC chains, sometimes culminating in a state of intense and painful feelings. Our bodies also develop physiological responses to these feedback loops such as increased heart rate, tightened muscles, and shorter breaths.

The core practice of CBT is being able to catch yourself as you are in an ABC chain so you can identify, challenge, and replace unhelpful automatic thoughts and prevent feedback loops from escalating.

CHANGING OUR THOUGHTS

The journaling exercises presented here help you understand your ABC chains and practice reframing your distorted and unhelpful thoughts. They are based on the CBT thought log (also known as a "thought record" or "thought diary"), a tool that is typically used alongside other CBT interventions with a licensed clinician. Although it isn't a replacement for sustained work with a therapist, the skills embedded in this journal can be learned on your own or in conjunction with the work you are doing in therapy. Be patient with yourself as you become familiar with the step-by-step structure of the journal entries. The skill of reframing can take several weeks to learn, even with the help of a therapist; it is normal for change to happen over time rather than right away.

Initially, these journal entries may work better as a reflection: consider completing them a few hours later or the next day after a triggering event. With practice, you may find that you prefer to give yourself time to regroup before reflecting on the situation, or that you prefer to do a journal entry while it's still fresh on your mind.

Each journal entry asks you to respond to a set of five questions to help you build and hone your CBT skills. The following paragraphs provide a detailed explanation of how to approach each of these questions. The benefits of this journal are realized through regular practice. While you will never be without negative automatic thoughts (we are human after all), over time you will notice that more helpful, realistic, and positive thoughts come to mind in response to an event. This will help you feel better and give you a better sense of control over your thoughts and feelings.

1   *What happened?*

Identify the activating situation. This helps you understand the entire ABC chain and learn to anticipate your situational triggers and patterns. When writing the description of the activating situation, be brief and focus on specific facts. The smaller the moment in time that you examine, the more effectively you'll be able to understand your emotions and reactions. Try your best to maintain a sense of objectivity. It may help to think about how much of your description of the events would be supported by a neutral party.

Sometimes people struggle to identify the activating situation. Even if this is the case for you, you can still complete the journal entries. Simply do your best to respond to the other questions. With time and practice, you'll start to notice patterns in what your thoughts are reacting to. The practice of identifying and challenging cognitive distortions is useful with or without an identifiable activating situation.

2   *What was going through your mind?*

Write down the thoughts you had during and immediately after the activating situation. The first key step in CBT is carefully listening to and understanding your thoughts. Since automatic thoughts are registered so quickly by our minds, they can be especially difficult to observe. Try to listen to your internal dialogue by slowing it down in your mind and then recalling the thoughts you had immediately after the activating situation.

You may find that it's very difficult to identify any thoughts. When this happens, continue probing by considering if you had thoughts about yourself, another person, or your environment.

3   *What emotions were you feeling?*

After considering your thoughts, identify the emotions you had during and immediately after the activating event and rate their intensity. Pause to reflect on the relationship between these emotions and the thoughts you listed above. If you are having difficulty naming your feelings, try using the Feelings Wheel on page 28, or consider the physical sensations that arose and work backward. For example, noticing your heart rate increase and jaw clench could indicate anger or fear.

4   *What thought patterns do you recognize?*

Examine the thoughts you listed and identify the unhelpful automatic thought patterns (i.e., cognitive distortions). This helps to build awareness of your common thought patterns, challenge their validity, and reduce their emotional impact. It is likely that many cognitive distortions will be present in a single thought. If calling out the distortions feels overwhelming, take a step back from owning the thoughts ("my thoughts") and try to treat them as if they belonged to someone else.

5   *How can you think about the situation differently?*

Try to formulate a different perspective on the situation. Challenging your initial thoughts gives you the opportunity to compose alternative thoughts based on the available facts. These alternative thoughts will change the way you perceive situations and will therefore help you start feeling better too. Here are some helpful questions you can ask to form alternative thoughts:

- What evidence do you have? What is the most realistic conclusion to draw based on that evidence?

- When looking at this situation, what's the best possible outcome? What's the worst possible outcome? What's the most realistic outcome?

- What might be a new way to look at the situation so that the impact of your perspective is positive or neutral?

- What might someone who has your best interests in mind say about this situation?

- Imagine you have the ability to zoom out of this situation and see it from an outside perspective. How does the situation look now?

- Imagine you are sitting with a therapist and trying to think about this situation differently. Then imagine switching roles—you are now the therapist. What would you tell your client?

Cognitive Distortions

Cognitive distortions are automatic thought patterns that are inaccurate and reinforce negative thinking or emotions. When we fall prey to these distortions, we interpret situations and events as much worse than they actually are, which can lead to additional anxiety, stress, and other negative feelings. In most cases, we can counter a distortion by taking a second look at a situation and reframing it through a more accurate lens.

Psychiatrist and researcher Aaron Beck is credited with first proposing the theory behind cognitive distortions in the 1970s, and his student David Burns is credited with popularizing the common names of these distortions in the 1980s. In one of his books, Burns writes, "I suspect you will find that a great many of your negative feelings are in fact based on such thinking errors."[3]

In this section, we outline 12 of the most common cognitive distortions. Note that while many of them may seem similar to each other, they differ in subtle yet significant ways. More than one can apply to any given situation.

1   ALL OR NOTHING THINKING

Sometimes called "polarized thinking" or "black-and-white thinking," this cognitive distortion leads you to perceive things at the extremes by removing the middle ground. All or nothing thinking makes the assumption that there are only two possibilities in a given situation, often expressed in either/or terms. You may think of yourself or others as being either great or awful, hard-working or lazy, delightful or intolerable, when the most accurate judgment probably lies somewhere between the extremes.

Example:
"I ate ice cream today so I've ruined my diet completely."

Example of reframing:
"Even while dieting, I can have foods I enjoy purely for their taste."

2   BLAMING OTHERS

Unlike self-blaming (see number 11), this cognitive distortion involves holding other people entirely accountable for a negative outcome. If you feel like a bad situation must be the fault of someone else, then you are blaming others.

Example:
"Dinner got burned because Sam left the kitchen a mess and I couldn't find anything I needed."

Example of reframing:
"Sam left the kitchen a mess—I will talk to him about cleaning up after himself. But I could have also prepared what space and things I needed before starting dinner."

3   CATASTROPHIZING

Catastrophizing is thinking about disastrous possibilities based on a relatively small observation or event. It can lead to believing that the worst-case scenario is the one that will play out.

Example:
"I botched that part of the interview; they probably will go with someone more qualified than me. I'll never get a job in my field and my student debt will have been for nothing."

Example of reframing:
"I think I answered that question poorly in the interview, but I feel good about some other responses. Hopefully this works out, but I will still have options even if it doesn't."

4   EMOTIONAL REASONING

This distortion can be summed up as, "If I feel that way, it must be true." When engaged in emotional reasoning, you accept your emotional reaction as an automatic indicator of reality. In other words, emotional reasoning occurs when you believe that something is true because of your feelings about it.

Example:
"I feel angry. This waiter must be treating me unfairly."

Example of reframing:
"I've been feeling really tired and upset today because of a few things at work. I should probably take a walk or a few deep breaths."

5   FORTUNE TELLING

Fortune telling refers to making predictions about the future based on little or no evidence. Just as mind reading overestimates our ability to know what other people are thinking (see number 8), fortune telling overestimates our ability to know what will happen in the future.

Example:
"The last relationship only lasted two months...this one probably will, too."

Example of reframing:
"I'm going to do my best to do what I feel is right for this new relationship, regardless of how long it lasts."

6   LABELING

This cognitive distortion is an extension of overgeneralization (see number 10) that involves assigning a negative global judgment (i.e., about an entire person or thing) based on a small amount of evidence. These labels create inaccurate views of the people, places, and things around us.

Example:
"I sent the invite to the wrong person. I'm so stupid."

Example of reframing:
"Ugh, I made a mistake and sent the invite to the wrong person. I feel pretty embarrassed."

7   MAGNIFYING THE NEGATIVE

Also referred to as "filtering" or "tunnel vision," magnifying the negative is when we fixate on the negative parts of a situation. When we dwell on the negative, our fears, losses, and irritations become exaggerated in importance and the positive parts of the situation are not given fair consideration.

Example:
"I can't believe I included a typo in my email to HR, they are definitely going to reject my request."

Example of reframing:
"I had a typo in my email to HR, but my meaning is still clear."

8   MIND READING

Mind reading involves making assumptions about what others are thinking and feeling based on limited evidence. Though it is possible to have an idea of what others are thinking, these intuitions are often inaccurate because there are so many factors that influence the thoughts and feelings of others that we are not aware of.

Example:
"The cashier must think I'm some weirdo for wearing this outfit to the store."

Example of reframing:
"I feel a bit self-conscious of my outfit, but others may not notice or care."

9 MINIMIZING THE POSITIVE

Whereas magnifying the negative turns up the volume of anything bad, minimizing the positive actively reduces the volume of anything good. Specifically, this means not acknowledging the value or importance of the positive parts of a situation.

Example:
"Anybody could have done what I did, they're just being nice to compliment me for it."

Example of reframing:
"I did something that people find valuable and praiseworthy."

10 OVERGENERALIZATION

In overgeneralization, broad conclusions are drawn based on just one piece of evidence. This thought pattern is often based on the assumption that bad experiences from the past will repeat themselves when similar situations come up again. Overgeneralizations can often be identified by the presence of words that imply absolutes, such as "all," "none," "never," and "always."

Example:
"I always get nervous and screw up presentations."

Example of reframing:
"Presentations tend to make me feel nervous."

11 SELF-BLAMING

Sometimes known as "personalization," this distortion involves believing that you are entirely responsible for a negative situation, even for factors that are outside of your control. Self-blaming also tends to involve assuming that what other people do or say is a reaction to you.

Example:
"I was late to hanging out with my friend and ruined what would've otherwise been a good time."

Example of reframing:
"I wish I hadn't been late, but it happens sometimes and I'm not fully responsible for how she felt."

12 SHOULD STATEMENTS

Should statements reflect narrow and inflexible rules about how you and other people should behave. Specifically, they involve believing that people "should" or "must" act a certain way and if they do not, they are judged as faulty, wrong, or inadequate. This distortion imposes a set of expectations that will very likely not be met. You feel guilty when you break them and angry when others break them.

Example:
"I shouldn't have been so upset with her. I should have been more calm and understanding."

Example of reframing:
"It's understandable that I felt hurt and it is helpful to communicate that. Next time, I can try to approach the situation more calmly."

The Feelings Wheel

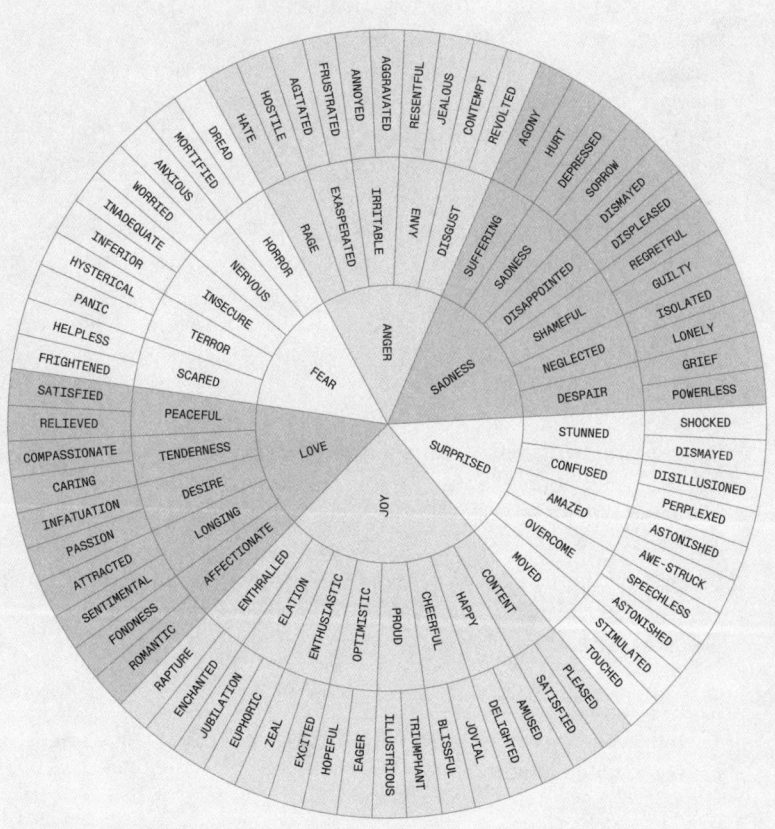

In your journal entries, you are tasked with listing your emotions and rating their intensity. But pinpointing emotions isn't a simple task. Within a feeling of happiness, you might also be experiencing something more specific, such as confidence, optimism, or gratitude. Or perhaps in a moment when you feel anxious, you decide after reflection that this feeling is best captured as a blend of frustration, rejection, and dismay. Having an accurate description of what you are feeling can greatly improve your ability to understand, communicate, and manage your emotional state.

The Feelings Wheel on the previous page is a tool used by therapists to help you quickly and accurately name the emotions you are feeling. The innermost ring of the wheel consists of six core emotions: joy, love, fear, anger, sadness, and surprise. The two outer rings include more detailed emotions associated with these core emotions.

To use the Feelings Wheel, start by scanning all three rings for an emotion that resonates with what you're feeling. Once you've identified that emotion, you can move toward or away from the center to test out related words and eventually settle on the one you think is most accurate for you. For instance, you might start with "sadness" and work outward to "guilty," or you might start with "nervous" and work your way inward to "fear," then outward again to "insecure." It may turn out that the emotion you pointed to first is the most accurate. That's fine. The idea is to test out a few so you can get a more nuanced sense of how you feel.

The goal is not to end up at any particular ring of the Feelings Wheel, though people do tend to gravitate toward the outer rings as they practice naming emotions. As you're getting started, simply focus on identifying and writing down the emotions that most clearly reflect your emotional state.

II Your Journal Entries

TIPS

- These journal entries are designed to be intuitive and easy to use. However, we recommend you peruse the CBT Basics, Cognitive Distortions, and Feelings Wheel sections in the Resource Guide and consult them as needed.

- The synthesis prompts that appear every 10 entries are provided to help you pause and reflect. What have you noticed? What connections are you making? We hope these breaks help you appreciate your increased awareness and growth.

- The purpose of this journal is to help you process your experiences in a constructive way. It is designed to give you full autonomy: you can start however you want and pick up whenever or wherever. We generally recommend using the journal entries when you feel anxious, stressed, depressed, or distressed. This will help you identify, track, and change patterns in your thinking.

Setting a specific intention can help guide you consciously and subconsciously. What unique purpose do you hope this journal will serve for you? What do you hope to get out of using it? Be as concrete or abstract as you'd like.

| JOURNAL ENTRY | GUIDE | | M | D | Y |

---

1   What happened?   (Describe the situation)

Identify the activating situation. Try to focus on the facts (who, what, when, where). Be brief and specific. The smaller the moment in time you can pinpoint, the better you'll understand the emotions and reactions that followed. "The boss called on me for an idea" is more effective than "monday morning meeting."

2   What was going through your mind?   (Describe your thoughts)

Write down the thoughts you had during and immediately after the activating situation. Identifying your thoughts is a foundational aspect of CBT. Instead of dismissing them (e.g., "it really wasn't that big of a deal"), allow them to flow honestly.

3   What emotions were you feeling?   (Note the intensity)

Name the emotions you felt and rate their intensity on a scale from 1   1 2 3 4 5 6 7 8 9 10

(barely feeling the emotion) to 10 (most intensely you've ever felt this   1 2 3 4 5 6 7 8 9 10

way). Use the Feelings Wheel in the Resource Guide for help.   1 2 3 4 5 6 7 8 9 10

| JOURNAL ENTRY | GUIDE | 35 |

4   What thought patterns do you recognize?   (Circle any or write your own)

All or nothing	Fortune telling	Minimizing the positive
Blaming others	Labeling	Overgeneralization
Catastrophizing	Magnifying the negative	Self-blaming
Emotional reasoning	Mind reading	Should statements

Examine the thoughts you listed and identify any unhelpful automatic thought patterns (i.e. cognitive distortions). Naming these distortions makes them less intimidating and helps to reduce their emotional impact. Consult the Cognitive Distortions section in the Resource Guide to see definitions of common patterns.

5   How can you think about the situation differently?   (Challenge your thoughts)

Formulate a new perspective on the situation. Taking a step back from automatically believing our thoughts is the hard work of CBT. Try to come up with a more objective, helpful, and nonjudgmental interpretation of the facts. What might a friend, mentor, or coach say? How can you grow from this? Consult the Resource Guide for more examples of how to reframe your thoughts.

JOURNAL ENTRY   GUIDE   36

This is your space. We encourage you to use it however you wish.

A few suggestions:

- Draw, sketch, scribble, or free write
- Continue your answers from the previous section
- Reflect on the therapist note on the next page
- List one small, concrete action you can take now or later that might make you feel better

NOTE FROM A THERAPIST

These notes will help guide your journaling, provide additional questions for reflection, or include tips for incorporating more tools into your life.

| JOURNAL ENTRY | SAMPLE ENTRY | M 01 | D 01 | Y 23 |

1 What happened? (Describe the situation)

At dinner, Jesse's mom made a joke about my job. Something about being an hourly worker. The whole family was there and everyone laughed.

2 What was going through your mind? (Describe your thoughts)

I immediately thought, why did she say that? Does everyone think I have a terrible job? I wondered if the entire family thinks I'm mooching off my partner's or that Jesse deserves better. Honestly, I thought maybe I really can't get a better job and Jesse might leave me eventually.

3 What emotions were you feeling? (Note the intensity)

Embarrassed   1 2 3 4 (5) 6 7 8 9 10
Self-Conscious   1 2 3 4 5 6 (7) 8 9 10
                       1 2 3 4 5 6 7 8 9 10

| 4 | What thought patterns do you recognize? | (Circle any or write your own) |

- All or nothing
- **Blaming others** ⃝
- Catastrophizing
- Emotional reasoning
- **Fortune telling** ⃝
- Labeling
- **Magnifying the negative** ⃝
- Mind reading
- Minimizing the positive
- Overgeneralization
- Self-blaming
- **Should statements** ⃝

| 5 | How can you think about the situation differently? | (Challenge your thoughts) |

Jesse's mom's comment hurt, but was likely just a joke without bad intentions. And though I do make less than Jesse, I really enjoy my job. I don't really know what Jesse's family thinks of me, but they consistently welcome me into their home and are friendly.

| JOURNAL ENTRY | SAMPLE ENTRY | M 01 | D 01 | Y 23 |

These moments are usually pretty tough for me. I know I spiral and they seem to happen a lot. I wonder if I should just talk to Jesse's mom about how I feel.

Next time I'll head to the bathroom, splash a little cold water on my face, and focus on my breathing for a minute.

NOTE FROM A THERAPIST

One helpful way to look at a situation differently is to think about it from the perspective of a friend.

Entries 1-10

II YOUR JOURNAL ENTRIES

| JOURNAL ENTRY | 001 | | M | D | Y |

1   What happened?   (Describe the situation)

2   What was going through your mind?   (Describe your thoughts)

3   What emotions were you feeling?   (Note the intensity)

1 2 3 4 5 6 7 8 9 10
1 2 3 4 5 6 7 8 9 10
1 2 3 4 5 6 7 8 9 10

JOURNAL ENTRY   001   45

| 4 | What thought patterns do you recognize? | (Circle any or write your own) |

    All or nothing   Fortune telling   Minimizing the positive
    Blaming others   Labeling   Overgeneralization
    Catastrophizing   Magnifying the negative   Self-blaming
    Emotional reasoning   Mind reading   Should statements

| 5 | How can you think about the situation differently? | (Challenge your thoughts) |

| JOURNAL ENTRY | 001 | | M | D | Y |

NOTE FROM A THERAPIST

How much of your time and energy are spent avoiding uncomfortable thoughts, feelings, or sensations? What might be contributing to this?

JOURNAL ENTRY　　002　　　　　　　　　　　　　　　　　　　　　| M　　| D　　| Y

1　　What happened?　　　　　　　　　　　　　　　　　　　　(Describe the situation)

2　　What was going through your mind?　　　　　　　　　　　(Describe your thoughts)

3　　What emotions were you feeling?　　　　　　　　　　　　　(Note the intensity)

　　　　　　　　　　　　　　　　　　　　　　　　　1 2 3 4 5 6 7 8 9 10
　　　　　　　　　　　　　　　　　　　　　　　　　1 2 3 4 5 6 7 8 9 10
　　　　　　　　　　　　　　　　　　　　　　　　　1 2 3 4 5 6 7 8 9 10

| 4 | What thought patterns do you recognize? | (Circle any or write your own) |

- All or nothing
- Blaming others
- Catastrophizing
- Emotional reasoning
- Fortune telling
- Labeling
- Magnifying the negative
- Mind reading
- Minimizing the positive
- Overgeneralization
- Self-blaming
- Should statements

| 5 | How can you think about the situation differently? | (Challenge your thoughts) |

JOURNAL ENTRY 002 | M | D | Y

NOTE FROM A THERAPIST

What are the moments or situations in which your mind feels calm or quiet?

| JOURNAL ENTRY | 003 | | M | D | Y |

1   What happened? (Describe the situation)

2   What was going through your mind? (Describe your thoughts)

3   What emotions were you feeling? (Note the intensity)

1 2 3 4 5 6 7 8 9 10
1 2 3 4 5 6 7 8 9 10
1 2 3 4 5 6 7 8 9 10

| JOURNAL ENTRY 003 | 53 |

4   What thought patterns do you recognize?   (Circle any or write your own)

All or nothing	Fortune telling	Minimizing the positive
Blaming others	Labeling	Overgeneralization
Catastrophizing	Magnifying the negative	Self-blaming
Emotional reasoning	Mind reading	Should statements

5   How can you think about the situation differently?   (Challenge your thoughts)

JOURNAL ENTRY 003 | M | D | Y

NOTE FROM A THERAPIST

Remember a time you felt confident and authentic.
What factors contributed to that moment?

| JOURNAL ENTRY | 004 | | M | D | Y |

1   What happened?   (Describe the situation)

2   What was going through your mind?   (Describe your thoughts)

3   What emotions were you feeling?   (Note the intensity)

1 2 3 4 5 6 7 8 9 10

1 2 3 4 5 6 7 8 9 10

1 2 3 4 5 6 7 8 9 10

| 4 | What thought patterns do you recognize? | (Circle any or write your own) |

All or nothing Fortune telling Minimizing the positive
Blaming others Labeling Overgeneralization
Catastrophizing Magnifying the negative Self-blaming
Emotional reasoning Mind reading Should statements

| 5 | How can you think about the situation differently? | (Challenge your thoughts) |

JOURNAL ENTRY 004 | M | D | Y

NOTE FROM A THERAPIST

How long does it take for you to react to a thought after thinking it? What might you do to delay the reaction by just a little bit?

| JOURNAL ENTRY | 005 | | M | D | Y |

1   What happened? (Describe the situation)

2   What was going through your mind? (Describe your thoughts)

3   What emotions were you feeling? (Note the intensity)

1 2 3 4 5 6 7 8 9 10
1 2 3 4 5 6 7 8 9 10
1 2 3 4 5 6 7 8 9 10

| 4 | What thought patterns do you recognize? | (Circle any or write your own) |

All or nothing
Blaming others
Catastrophizing
Emotional reasoning

Fortune telling
Labeling
Magnifying the negative
Mind reading

Minimizing the positive
Overgeneralization
Self-blaming
Should statements

| 5 | How can you think about the situation differently? | (Challenge your thoughts) |

JOURNAL ENTRY 005 | M | D | Y

NOTE FROM A THERAPIST

When we're feeling stuck, it can be helpful to challenge our habitual ways of doing things in order to make space for bigger changes. Examples could include redecorating a room, breaking up a morning routine, or doing anything that shakes up our patterns. What's something you recently did differently?

| JOURNAL ENTRY | 006 | | M | D | Y |

1   What happened? (Describe the situation)

2   What was going through your mind? (Describe your thoughts)

3   What emotions were you feeling? (Note the intensity)

1 2 3 4 5 6 7 8 9 10
1 2 3 4 5 6 7 8 9 10
1 2 3 4 5 6 7 8 9 10

| 4 | What thought patterns do you recognize? | (Circle any or write your own) |

All or nothing
Blaming others
Catastrophizing
Emotional reasoning

Fortune telling
Labeling
Magnifying the negative
Mind reading

Minimizing the positive
Overgeneralization
Self-blaming
Should statements

| 5 | How can you think about the situation differently? | (Challenge your thoughts) |

JOURNAL ENTRY 006 | M | D | Y

NOTE FROM A THERAPIST

Multitasking, or rapidly switching between tasks, can lead to cognitive fatigue, which exacerbates negative thought patterns. Consider the last time you tried to juggle many tasks at once. How did it affect your energy and productivity?

| JOURNAL ENTRY | 007 | | M | D | Y |

1. What happened? (Describe the situation)

2. What was going through your mind? (Describe your thoughts)

3. What emotions were you feeling? (Note the intensity)

1 2 3 4 5 6 7 8 9 10
1 2 3 4 5 6 7 8 9 10
1 2 3 4 5 6 7 8 9 10

| 4 | What thought patterns do you recognize? | (Circle any or write your own) |

All or nothing Fortune telling Minimizing the positive
Blaming others Labeling Overgeneralization
Catastrophizing Magnifying the negative Self-blaming
Emotional reasoning Mind reading Should statements

| 5 | How can you think about the situation differently? | (Challenge your thoughts) |

| JOURNAL ENTRY | 007 | M | D | Y |

NOTE FROM A THERAPIST

As you learn to catch and reframe your thoughts, try to be gentle with yourself and curious about the process. You are gradually building an awareness of thought patterns that are difficult to recognize.

| JOURNAL ENTRY | 008 | | M | D | Y |

1 What happened? (Describe the situation)

2 What was going through your mind? (Describe your thoughts)

3 What emotions were you feeling? (Note the intensity)

1 2 3 4 5 6 7 8 9 10
1 2 3 4 5 6 7 8 9 10
1 2 3 4 5 6 7 8 9 10

4	What thought patterns do you recognize?	(Circle any or write your own)

All or nothing	Fortune telling	Minimizing the positive
Blaming others	Labeling	Overgeneralization
Catastrophizing	Magnifying the negative	Self-blaming
Emotional reasoning	Mind reading	Should statements

5	How can you think about the situation differently?	(Challenge your thoughts)

JOURNAL ENTRY 008 | M | D | Y

NOTE FROM A THERAPIST

Think about your most common or "go-to" feelings. Hiding behind these, are there deeper feelings that you feel less comfortable naming (such as guilt, shame, resentment, or hopelessness)?

| JOURNAL ENTRY | 009 | | M | D | Y |

1   What happened?   (Describe the situation)

2   What was going through your mind?   (Describe your thoughts)

3   What emotions were you feeling?   (Note the intensity)

1 2 3 4 5 6 7 8 9 10

1 2 3 4 5 6 7 8 9 10

1 2 3 4 5 6 7 8 9 10

JOURNAL ENTRY 009 — 77

| 4 | What thought patterns do you recognize? | (Circle any or write your own) |

- All or nothing
- Blaming others
- Catastrophizing
- Emotional reasoning
- Fortune telling
- Labeling
- Magnifying the negative
- Mind reading
- Minimizing the positive
- Overgeneralization
- Self-blaming
- Should statements

| 5 | How can you think about the situation differently? | (Challenge your thoughts) |

JOURNAL ENTRY 009 | M | D | Y

NOTE FROM A THERAPIST

Remember that the goal of reframing is not unconditional positivity. It's to make room for more nuance and uncertainty as you take a second look at the situation.

JOURNAL ENTRY   010 | M | D | Y

1   What happened?   (Describe the situation)

2   What was going through your mind?   (Describe your thoughts)

3   What emotions were you feeling?   (Note the intensity)

1 2 3 4 5 6 7 8 9 10
1 2 3 4 5 6 7 8 9 10
1 2 3 4 5 6 7 8 9 10

JOURNAL ENTRY 010

4   What thought patterns do you recognize?   (Circle any or write your own)

All or nothing	Fortune telling	Minimizing the positive
Blaming others	Labeling	Overgeneralization
Catastrophizing	Magnifying the negative	Self-blaming
Emotional reasoning	Mind reading	Should statements

5   How can you think about the situation differently?   (Challenge your thoughts)

JOURNAL ENTRY 010 | M | D | Y

NOTE FROM A THERAPIST

Tracking difficult moments can make it easy to minimize the positives. Consider some of the traits that are most important to you to embody (e.g., kindness, authenticity, justice) and ask yourself, "How did I exemplify one of these traits recently?"

JOURNAL SYNTHESIS

1 Page through Journal Entries 1 - 10. What patterns do you notice?

2 Do you notice that certain cognitive distortions lead to more distress?

3   What changes have you noticed in your ability to identify thought patterns and reframe your thoughts?

4   What's something you'd like to try and do differently, or continue doing, as you move on to Journal Entries 11 - 20?

Entries 11-20

II YOUR JOURNAL ENTRIES

| JOURNAL ENTRY | 011 | | M | D | Y |

1   What happened?   (Describe the situation)

2   What was going through your mind?   (Describe your thoughts)

3   What emotions were you feeling?   (Note the intensity)

1 2 3 4 5 6 7 8 9 10
1 2 3 4 5 6 7 8 9 10
1 2 3 4 5 6 7 8 9 10

| 4 | What thought patterns do you recognize? | (Circle any or write your own) |

All or nothing	Fortune telling	Minimizing the positive
Blaming others	Labeling	Overgeneralization
Catastrophizing	Magnifying the negative	Self-blaming
Emotional reasoning	Mind reading	Should statements

| 5 | How can you think about the situation differently? | (Challenge your thoughts) |

JOURNAL ENTRY 011 | M | D | Y

NOTE FROM A THERAPIST

Hold your hands to your heart and apply enough pressure to feel your heartbeat in your palm. How would you describe this sensation?

| JOURNAL ENTRY | 012 | | M | D | Y |

1 What happened? (Describe the situation)

2 What was going through your mind? (Describe your thoughts)

3 What emotions were you feeling? (Note the intensity)

1 2 3 4 5 6 7 8 9 10
1 2 3 4 5 6 7 8 9 10
1 2 3 4 5 6 7 8 9 10

| 4 | What thought patterns do you recognize? | (Circle any or write your own) |

- All or nothing
- Blaming others
- Catastrophizing
- Emotional reasoning
- Fortune telling
- Labeling
- Magnifying the negative
- Mind reading
- Minimizing the positive
- Overgeneralization
- Self-blaming
- Should statements

| 5 | How can you think about the situation differently? | (Challenge your thoughts) |

JOURNAL ENTRY 012 | M | D | Y

NOTE FROM A THERAPIST

Some distressing thoughts are so repetitive and frequent that we know they're untrue. The next time you notice one of these thoughts forming, try imagining a stop sign and telling yourself, "STOP."

| JOURNAL ENTRY | 013 | | M | D | Y |

1 What happened? (Describe the situation)

2 What was going through your mind? (Describe your thoughts)

3 What emotions were you feeling? (Note the intensity)

1 2 3 4 5 6 7 8 9 10
1 2 3 4 5 6 7 8 9 10
1 2 3 4 5 6 7 8 9 10

| 4 | What thought patterns do you recognize? | (Circle any or write your own) |

All or nothing
Blaming others
Catastrophizing
Emotional reasoning

Fortune telling
Labeling
Magnifying the negative
Mind reading

Minimizing the positive
Overgeneralization
Self-blaming
Should statements

| 5 | How can you think about the situation differently? | (Challenge your thoughts) |

JOURNAL ENTRY 013 | M | D | Y

NOTE FROM A THERAPIST

Journaling may be a solitary pursuit, but you can always bring others into the CBT process. Are there people in your life who can help you identify and challenge cognitive distortions?

| JOURNAL ENTRY | 014 | | M | D | Y |

1 What happened? (Describe the situation)

2 What was going through your mind? (Describe your thoughts)

3 What emotions were you feeling? (Note the intensity)

1 2 3 4 5 6 7 8 9 10
1 2 3 4 5 6 7 8 9 10
1 2 3 4 5 6 7 8 9 10

| 4 | What thought patterns do you recognize? | (Circle any or write your own) |

All or nothing	Fortune telling	Minimizing the positive
Blaming others	Labeling	Overgeneralization
Catastrophizing	Magnifying the negative	Self-blaming
Emotional reasoning	Mind reading	Should statements

| 5 | How can you think about the situation differently? | (Challenge your thoughts) |

JOURNAL ENTRY 014 | M | D | Y

NOTE FROM A THERAPIST

Consider the steps you've taken to improve your mental health. These may involve physical self-care, social connections, or even the journal entries in this book. Give yourself kudos for putting in this effort.

| JOURNAL ENTRY | 015 | | M | D | Y |

1. What happened? *(Describe the situation)*

2. What was going through your mind? *(Describe your thoughts)*

3. What emotions were you feeling? *(Note the intensity)*

1 2 3 4 5 6 7 8 9 10
1 2 3 4 5 6 7 8 9 10
1 2 3 4 5 6 7 8 9 10

4 — What thought patterns do you recognize? (Circle any or write your own)

- All or nothing
- Blaming others
- Catastrophizing
- Emotional reasoning
- Fortune telling
- Labeling
- Magnifying the negative
- Mind reading
- Minimizing the positive
- Overgeneralization
- Self-blaming
- Should statements

5 — How can you think about the situation differently? (Challenge your thoughts)

JOURNAL ENTRY 015 | M | D | Y

NOTE FROM A THERAPIST

Think of a few expectations or "shoulds" that have been put on you by others. What are the risks and benefits of challenging these beliefs?

| JOURNAL ENTRY | 016 | | M | D | Y |

1 What happened? (Describe the situation)

2 What was going through your mind? (Describe your thoughts)

3 What emotions were you feeling? (Note the intensity)

1 2 3 4 5 6 7 8 9 10
1 2 3 4 5 6 7 8 9 10
1 2 3 4 5 6 7 8 9 10

| 4 | What thought patterns do you recognize? | (Circle any or write your own) |

All or nothing	Fortune telling	Minimizing the positive
Blaming others	Labeling	Overgeneralization
Catastrophizing	Magnifying the negative	Self-blaming
Emotional reasoning	Mind reading	Should statements

| 5 | How can you think about the situation differently? | (Challenge your thoughts) |

JOURNAL ENTRY 016

NOTE FROM A THERAPIST

What types of situations do you turn to these journal entries for? What makes them especially helpful for those moments?

| JOURNAL ENTRY | 017 | M | D | Y |

1   What happened?   (Describe the situation)

2   What was going through your mind?   (Describe your thoughts)

3   What emotions were you feeling?   (Note the intensity)

                                                         1 2 3 4 5 6 7 8 9 10

                                                         1 2 3 4 5 6 7 8 9 10

                                                         1 2 3 4 5 6 7 8 9 10

| 4 | What thought patterns do you recognize? | (Circle any or write your own) |

- All or nothing
- Blaming others
- Catastrophizing
- Emotional reasoning
- Fortune telling
- Labeling
- Magnifying the negative
- Mind reading
- Minimizing the positive
- Overgeneralization
- Self-blaming
- Should statements

| 5 | How can you think about the situation differently? | (Challenge your thoughts) |

JOURNAL ENTRY 017

NOTE FROM A THERAPIST

Worrying often happens when we overextend our perception of control. This can feel productive, but we end up consuming time and energy over something that we can't actually change. The next time you notice yourself worrying, ask what about the situation is truly within your control and what you would like to do about it.

| JOURNAL ENTRY | 018 | | M | D | Y |

1. What happened?
(Describe the situation)

2. What was going through your mind?
(Describe your thoughts)

3. What emotions were you feeling?
(Note the intensity)

1 2 3 4 5 6 7 8 9 10
1 2 3 4 5 6 7 8 9 10
1 2 3 4 5 6 7 8 9 10

| 4 | What thought patterns do you recognize? | (Circle any or write your own) |

All or nothing
Blaming others
Catastrophizing
Emotional reasoning

Fortune telling
Labeling
Magnifying the negative
Mind reading

Minimizing the positive
Overgeneralization
Self-blaming
Should statements

| 5 | How can you think about the situation differently? | (Challenge your thoughts) |

JOURNAL ENTRY 018 | M | D | Y

NOTE FROM A THERAPIST

Look up from the page at your surroundings. How would you describe their details to someone who cannot see them? Doing so often means moving away from judgments or generalizations.

| JOURNAL ENTRY | 019 | | M | D | Y |

---

1 What happened? — (Describe the situation)

2 What was going through your mind? (Describe your thoughts)

3 What emotions were you feeling? (Note the intensity)

1 2 3 4 5 6 7 8 9 10
1 2 3 4 5 6 7 8 9 10
1 2 3 4 5 6 7 8 9 10

| 4 | What thought patterns do you recognize? | (Circle any or write your own) |

- All or nothing
- Blaming others
- Catastrophizing
- Emotional reasoning
- Fortune telling
- Labeling
- Magnifying the negative
- Mind reading
- Minimizing the positive
- Overgeneralization
- Self-blaming
- Should statements

| 5 | How can you think about the situation differently? | (Challenge your thoughts) |

JOURNAL ENTRY 019 | M | D | Y

NOTE FROM A THERAPIST

Some ideas we have about ourselves can feel like permanent truths, even though they are actually subject to change. What are some of your thoughts like this?

| JOURNAL ENTRY | 020 | | M | D | Y |

1 What happened? *(Describe the situation)*

2 What was going through your mind? *(Describe your thoughts)*

3 What emotions were you feeling? *(Note the intensity)*

1 2 3 4 5 6 7 8 9 10

1 2 3 4 5 6 7 8 9 10

1 2 3 4 5 6 7 8 9 10

| 4 | What thought patterns do you recognize? | (Circle any or write your own) |

All or nothing Fortune telling Minimizing the positive
Blaming others Labeling Overgeneralization
Catastrophizing Magnifying the negative Self-blaming
Emotional reasoning Mind reading Should statements

| 5 | How can you think about the situation differently? | (Challenge your thoughts) |

JOURNAL ENTRY 020 | M | D | Y

NOTE FROM A THERAPIST

There is no perfect way to respond to a situation. Remember to let yourself be human—with all the flaws and imperfections that come with it—as you move toward change.

II   JOURNAL SYNTHESIS

1   Page through Journal Entries 11 - 20. What patterns do you notice?

2   Do you notice that certain cognitive distortions lead to more distress?

JOURNAL SYNTHESIS

3 What changes have you noticed in your ability to identify thought patterns and reframe your thoughts?

4 What's something you'd like to try and do differently, or continue doing, as you move on to Journal Entries 21 - 30?

Entries 21-30

YOUR JOURNAL ENTRIES

| JOURNAL ENTRY | 021 | | M | D | Y |

1   What happened?   (Describe the situation)

2   What was going through your mind?   (Describe your thoughts)

3   What emotions were you feeling?   (Note the intensity)

1 2 3 4 5 6 7 8 9 10
1 2 3 4 5 6 7 8 9 10
1 2 3 4 5 6 7 8 9 10

| 4 | What thought patterns do you recognize? | (Circle any or write your own) |

All or nothing   Fortune telling   Minimizing the positive
Blaming others   Labeling   Overgeneralization
Catastrophizing   Magnifying the negative   Self-blaming
Emotional reasoning   Mind reading   Should statements

| 5 | How can you think about the situation differently? | (Challenge your thoughts) |

JOURNAL ENTRY 021 | M | D | Y

NOTE FROM A THERAPIST

It can feel overwhelming to consider the big picture. Try to zoom in on the present moment. What are one or two actionable steps you can focus on?

| JOURNAL ENTRY | 022 | M | D | Y |

1   What happened? (Describe the situation)

2   What was going through your mind? (Describe your thoughts)

3   What emotions were you feeling? (Note the intensity)

1 2 3 4 5 6 7 8 9 10
1 2 3 4 5 6 7 8 9 10
1 2 3 4 5 6 7 8 9 10

| 4 | What thought patterns do you recognize? | (Circle any or write your own) |

All or nothing   Fortune telling   Minimizing the positive
Blaming others   Labeling   Overgeneralization
Catastrophizing   Magnifying the negative   Self-blaming
Emotional reasoning   Mind reading   Should statements

| 5 | How can you think about the situation differently? | (Challenge your thoughts) |

JOURNAL ENTRY 022 | M | D | Y

NOTE FROM A THERAPIST

What are the fears that make you feel stuck in a situation or unable to make changes? Recognize that any time you challenge these fears is a big step forward.

| JOURNAL ENTRY | 023 | | M | D | Y |

1   What happened?   (Describe the situation)

2   What was going through your mind?   (Describe your thoughts)

3   What emotions were you feeling?   (Note the intensity)

1 2 3 4 5 6 7 8 9 10
1 2 3 4 5 6 7 8 9 10
1 2 3 4 5 6 7 8 9 10

| 4 | What thought patterns do you recognize? | (Circle any or write your own) |

All or nothing
Blaming others
Catastrophizing
Emotional reasoning

Fortune telling
Labeling
Magnifying the negative
Mind reading

Minimizing the positive
Overgeneralization
Self-blaming
Should statements

| 5 | How can you think about the situation differently? | (Challenge your thoughts) |

JOURNAL ENTRY 023 | M | D | Y

NOTE FROM A THERAPIST

Sometimes our "should" thoughts can make normal behaviors feel wrong, especially when we compare ourselves to other people. (For example: "I should be working this weekend instead of traveling. All my friends work harder than me.")
What comparisons are leading to your "should" thoughts?

| JOURNAL ENTRY | 024 | | M | D | Y |

1   What happened?   (Describe the situation)

2   What was going through your mind?   (Describe your thoughts)

3   What emotions were you feeling?   (Note the intensity)

1 2 3 4 5 6 7 8 9 10
1 2 3 4 5 6 7 8 9 10
1 2 3 4 5 6 7 8 9 10

| 4 | What thought patterns do you recognize? | (Circle any or write your own) |

All or nothing
Blaming others
Catastrophizing
Emotional reasoning

Fortune telling
Labeling
Magnifying the negative
Mind reading

Minimizing the positive
Overgeneralization
Self-blaming
Should statements

| 5 | How can you think about the situation differently? | (Challenge your thoughts) |

JOURNAL ENTRY 024 | M | D | Y

NOTE FROM A THERAPIST

Our thoughts and feelings are inextricably tied to our physical health. How are you doing today in fulfilling your basic physical needs—things like eating, hydrating, moving, and resting?

| JOURNAL ENTRY | 025 | | M | D | Y |

1   What happened?   (Describe the situation)

2   What was going through your mind?   (Describe your thoughts)

3   What emotions were you feeling?   (Note the intensity)

1 2 3 4 5 6 7 8 9 10

1 2 3 4 5 6 7 8 9 10

1 2 3 4 5 6 7 8 9 10

| 4 | What thought patterns do you recognize? | (Circle any or write your own) |

- All or nothing
- Blaming others
- Catastrophizing
- Emotional reasoning
- Fortune telling
- Labeling
- Magnifying the negative
- Mind reading
- Minimizing the positive
- Overgeneralization
- Self-blaming
- Should statements

| 5 | How can you think about the situation differently? | (Challenge your thoughts) |

JOURNAL ENTRY 025 | M | D | Y

NOTE FROM A THERAPIST

You might find yourself asking, "Why do I keep thinking or feeling this way?" Sometimes this can be because these patterns keep us from feeling bad in other ways. What ongoing difficulties might your patterns be helping you avoid or ignore?

| JOURNAL ENTRY | 026 | | M | D | Y |

1   What happened? (Describe the situation)

2   What was going through your mind? (Describe your thoughts)

3   What emotions were you feeling? (Note the intensity)

1 2 3 4 5 6 7 8 9 10
1 2 3 4 5 6 7 8 9 10
1 2 3 4 5 6 7 8 9 10

| 4 | What thought patterns do you recognize? | (Circle any or write your own) |

- All or nothing
- Blaming others
- Catastrophizing
- Emotional reasoning
- Fortune telling
- Labeling
- Magnifying the negative
- Mind reading
- Minimizing the positive
- Overgeneralization
- Self-blaming
- Should statements

| 5 | How can you think about the situation differently? | (Challenge your thoughts) |

JOURNAL ENTRY 026 | M | D | Y

NOTE FROM A THERAPIST

It's common for us to feel bad about a situation—"I sent the incorrect email to my boss"—and simultaneously feel bad about how we feel—"I can't believe I'm getting so worked up about this!" What are some thoughts and judgments that you have about your feelings?

| JOURNAL ENTRY | 027 | | M | D | Y |

1   What happened?   (Describe the situation)

2   What was going through your mind?   (Describe your thoughts)

3   What emotions were you feeling?   (Note the intensity)

1 2 3 4 5 6 7 8 9 10

1 2 3 4 5 6 7 8 9 10

1 2 3 4 5 6 7 8 9 10

| 4 | What thought patterns do you recognize? | (Circle any or write your own) |

    All or nothing   Fortune telling   Minimizing the positive
    Blaming others   Labeling   Overgeneralization
    Catastrophizing   Magnifying the negative   Self-blaming
    Emotional reasoning   Mind reading   Should statements

| 5 | How can you think about the situation differently? | (Challenge your thoughts) |

JOURNAL ENTRY 027 | M | D | Y

NOTE FROM A THERAPIST

We sometimes use substances (such as coffee or alcohol) when we have thoughts or feelings we dislike. But in many cases, these substances work because of the placebo effect. If this were true for you, would it change your approach to substances? How so?

| JOURNAL ENTRY | 028 | | M | D | Y |

1   What happened?   (Describe the situation)

2   What was going through your mind?   (Describe your thoughts)

3   What emotions were you feeling?   (Note the intensity)

1 2 3 4 5 6 7 8 9 10
1 2 3 4 5 6 7 8 9 10
1 2 3 4 5 6 7 8 9 10

| 4 | What thought patterns do you recognize? | (Circle any or write your own) |

- All or nothing
- Blaming others
- Catastrophizing
- Emotional reasoning
- Fortune telling
- Labeling
- Magnifying the negative
- Mind reading
- Minimizing the positive
- Overgeneralization
- Self-blaming
- Should statements

| 5 | How can you think about the situation differently? | (Challenge your thoughts) |

JOURNAL ENTRY 028 | M | D | Y

NOTE FROM A THERAPIST

What's your most common cognitive distortion? How would you explain this distortion to a friend?

| JOURNAL ENTRY | 029 | | M | D | Y |

1   What happened? (Describe the situation)

2   What was going through your mind? (Describe your thoughts)

3   What emotions were you feeling? (Note the intensity)

1 2 3 4 5 6 7 8 9 10
1 2 3 4 5 6 7 8 9 10
1 2 3 4 5 6 7 8 9 10

| 4 | What thought patterns do you recognize? | (Circle any or write your own) |

- All or nothing
- Blaming others
- Catastrophizing
- Emotional reasoning
- Fortune telling
- Labeling
- Magnifying the negative
- Mind reading
- Minimizing the positive
- Overgeneralization
- Self-blaming
- Should statements

| 5 | How can you think about the situation differently? | (Challenge your thoughts) |

JOURNAL ENTRY 029 | M | D | Y

NOTE FROM A THERAPIST

Let yourself be still for a moment. What thoughts, feelings, or sensations come to the forefront in this stillness?

| JOURNAL ENTRY | 030 | | M | D | Y |

1 What happened? (Describe the situation)

2 What was going through your mind? (Describe your thoughts)

3 What emotions were you feeling? (Note the intensity)

1 2 3 4 5 6 7 8 9 10
1 2 3 4 5 6 7 8 9 10
1 2 3 4 5 6 7 8 9 10

| 4 | What thought patterns do you recognize? | (Circle any or write your own) |

- All or nothing
- Blaming others
- Catastrophizing
- Emotional reasoning
- Fortune telling
- Labeling
- Magnifying the negative
- Mind reading
- Minimizing the positive
- Overgeneralization
- Self-blaming
- Should statements

| 5 | How can you think about the situation differently? | (Challenge your thoughts) |

JOURNAL ENTRY 030 | M | D | Y

NOTE FROM A THERAPIST

We often have judgments about our emotions. (For example: "I shouldn't feel this way" or "Other people wouldn't have this feeling.") What judgments prevent you from accepting it?

1   Page through Journal Entries 21 - 30. What patterns do you notice?

2   Do you notice that certain cognitive distortions lead to more distress?

3   What changes have you noticed in your ability to identify thought patterns and reframe your thoughts?

4   What's something you'd like to try and do differently, or continue doing, as you move beyond this journal?

References

[1] David, D., Cristea, I., & Hofmann, S. G. (2018). Why cognitive behavioral therapy is the current gold standard of psychotherapy. Frontiers in Psychiatry, 9, 4.
▸ *https://doi.org/10.3389/fpsyt.2018.00004*

[2] Hofmann, S. G., Asnaani, A., Vonk, I.J., Sawyer, A.T., & Fang, A. (2012). The efficacy of cognitive behavioral therapy: A review of meta-analyses. Cognitive Therapy and Research, 36(5), 427–440. ▸ *https://doi.org/10.1007/s10608-012-9476-1*

[3] Burns, D. D. (1999). *The feeling good handbook* (Rev. ed.). Plume.

NOTES